PRAISE F(

While these people :
is what we THINK they would pre-
about David's book, "Rock Star: Finding God's
Purpose for Your Life".

"The magic tapestry that you wove into a ma-
jor part of my life story was pure of heart and
filled with truth, like a chalice overflowing!
Bravo Sir David! Well written my namesake!"
~ King David

"Without rocks and deserts and mountains to
climb, where would I have gone to experience
God? Rocks, and slabs of stone of course, are
some of my favorites of God's creation. The
fact that you chose a rock, to be the star of
your book, tells me that we all need to see the
beauty in the seemingly mundane around us. In
this book, "The Rock", lived a life of exciting
purpose and great patience. May we all be so
blessed." ~ Moses

"Now that's a story of faith! I remember when
I was told to build my ark, I thought I must be
hearing things! Actually wondered about my
own sanity! And now, reading about that little
rock in your book "Rock Star", and the perse-

verance that boy had, kind of reminds me, of me at his age! I'd want that li' fella on my side in any trial in life. Great book, son!" ~Noah

"As my brother and sister monks read your book, we saw the truth behind the thought, that yes life is a struggle. We also acknowledge the compassion for self that our friend "The Rock" has, and how this compassion can be the key to freedom, to purpose. We also believe, and giggled in unison as we share, that he would look just beautiful in a yellow robe. " ~Buddha

"Being unsure of our worthiness is something I struggled with my whole life! How I could relate to the beautiful main character of your book David! As I came to the understanding of the love God had for me my entire life, regardless of what others thought, I too found my purpose." ~ Mary Magdalene

"The spirit inside "The Rock" in your heavenly book, David, is the light inside each of you. I see it so clearly, that no one amongst you is ever to be left behind. While everyone goes through their 40 days and 40 nights seemingly on their own in the desert, you are not alone. I am right beside you, just as so warmly shared here, encouraging you to dig your way back to the light, the presence of the Father, who will so surely guide you to the path to serve. As it is, so it shall be. Forever and ever. Amen." ~ Jesus of Nazareth

What other "Rock Stars" have to say about David Essel and some of his other work...

"David Essel's destiny is to help you become more alive in every area of your life." ~ Wayne W. Dyer, best selling author

"I love it! You are very talented, bright and insightful!" ~Jenna Elfman, Actress, TV Star, on David's book "Phoenix Soul"

"David is the radiant soul of radio, he's brilliant, insightful and easy to listen to. David Makes a real difference in his listener's lives." ~ Mark Victor Hansen, co-author, "Chicken Soup for the Soul"

"A feel good story giving life, humor and value to childhood's most important lessons: empathy, compassion, self confidence and connection. We need a whole series of books like this!" ~ Kenny Loggins, Singer/songwriter on David's children's book "Cat Calloway"

David Essel's Books

Rock Star: Finding God's Purpose for Your Life
(Print & e-Book)

Heaven On Earth: God Speaks Through the Heart of A Young Monk

Slow Down: The Fastest Way To Get Everything You Want

Phoenix Soul: One Man's Search for Love & Inner Peace

Language for the Heart & Soul: Powerful Writings on Life

The Real Life Adventures of Catherine "Cat" Calloway

David Essel's CD's & DVD's

SLOW DOWN: The Fastest Way to Get Everything You Want

(Live Presentation 3 CD Set)

SLOW DOWN: Awaken to Your Own Spiritual Path CD

SLOW DOWN: Shift Your Energy Through Meditation CD

SLOW DOWN: Transform Your Stress Into Success CD

REAL ESTATE CD by DAVID ESSEL (2 DISC CD)

THE POWER OF TRANSFORMATIONAL THINKING DVD

STEP TRAINING EXERCISE DVD – Beginner/Intermediate

ROCK STAR!

Finding God's Purpose for Your Life

By David Essel, M.S.

APPRECIATION

"I would love to thank God for the incredible gifts He has bestowed upon me and the many people in my life for their help in making this book a reality.

First, Homeless Mark, I pray he is safe and well today. My family, mom and dad, sister Marydiane and my brother Terry for their constant support of everything I do!

Caroline Ravelo, for taking my spoken manuscript, and turning it into a manageable product! To Renee Bledsoe for her internet expertise and guidance in the publishing process, who knew this had to be made available in e-book format, as well.

To Ardith and Tracy, Kim, Brad, Troy, Pat, and the many people who proofread the original manuscript, offering their support and input that made such a huge difference in the final copy that you are reading right now.

And to the many people from around the world who continue to support all of our work in the world of inspiration.

I thank you, and love you, all.

~ David

DEDICATION

I dedicate this book to Marydiane Scheemaker, who has been my loving and amazingly supportive sister through all the years of my life. Her work as an elementary school teacher, at our former grade school, St. Rose of Lima in North Syracuse, New York, has been a huge help in the formulation of my children's book "Cat Calloway", as well as in this one, "Rock Star".

I Love you, Sis!

PREFACE

This is the story of "Rock Star", one of the most amazing stories ever given, from God to man, about how incredible and unique we all are. Each of us has the Divine within. And yet, we are the only ones who can release this beauty as we express ourselves and find true meaning for our life.

I am so excited to share this story with you, and I know that it will make a huge difference in the lives of children, teens, young adults, adults and seniors around the world. The story you are about to read could be your own story.

Every person in the world is a "rock star" in the eyes of God, with a unique God given talent. Each of us stands on our own stage, the stage of our life. Isn't that an amazing thing to think about?

If I were to ask you right now, what makes you unique, what makes you special and different, what would you say? Did you know that no one before or after you will ever have the same fingerprints that you have? You are God's child, so beautiful, so special, that He has given

you a fingerprint that has never been dupli-
cated, and never will be!

When you look in the mirror and realize how
special you are, you will deeply connect with
the story that I am about to tell you. You see,
this story is the story of your life, if you want
it to be.

You can rise above mediocrity. You can rise
above that feeling that says, "I am no one special." You can rise above the thought that
many believe, "I have no special gifts". You
can rise above all of that through reading this
story, and see yourself, already as the "rock
star" in your life, the "rock star" God wants
you to be.

Yes! God wants you to see that you are the
"rock star" of the universe, in His eyes. And so
it is, and so it shall be.

INTRODUCTION

A number of years ago, while out for my daily run, I passed an area along the bay front where homeless people would congregate during the day.

Whenever I was walking in this area of town, I would be approached and asked for money. But I was never approached if I was running. Until this one very special day.

For on this day, as I was walking at the end of my run, with money in my pocket, (and I never carried money with me on the days I ran), a homeless person came up and wanted to talk to me.

This gentleman was someone I had seen on numerous occasions. As I strolled through the parking lot, all of a sudden I heard, "Sir! Sir! Excuse me! Excuse me!" and he started walking towards me.

I looked at him and said, "Hey! It's really good to see you."

He looked a little astonished. He looked as if he'd never seen me before, even though we had seen each other here several times in the past.

He said, "Thank you. I need money to get a bus ticket out of this area, back to my brother's where I can get a job. Is there any way you could spare me some money?"

Now, this was a very similar story that I had heard from this person before. I just had to chuckle inside. It was the same thing all the time. I could smell alcohol on his breath. He had very few teeth in his mouth. He looked probably twenty-years older than his real age. In other words, the addiction to alcohol had taken over his body.

As I looked into his eyes, I said, "I don't normally carry any money when I'm out running." As I put my hand in my pocket, I was surprised to feel what I thought was a dollar bill there.

He then said, "Well, you know, I'm just trying to get this bus ticket home, and if I could just get a bus ticket, I could get a job, and …" He went on with his story. It was always the same story, and he was always in the same parking lot, so he either never got enough money to get out of the city or he was using the money for his addiction.

I pulled out what I thought was a one dollar bill. But, when I looked at it closer, I saw that it was a five dollar bill!

Now, I have to tell you, at that moment, I wanted to put my hand back in my pocket. I really did. I did not want to give this person a five dollar bill. I wouldn't have minded giving a dollar, two dollars or even three, but there was something about a five dollar bill that I didn't feel comfortable with.

Now, let me back-up a little bit here. Over the years, prior to this experience, I had met many homeless people in my life. As a matter of fact, I had been interviewed on nationally syndicated TV shows about the homeless. I was also the guest host on a radio show in a city in Texas, where we focused on the struggles of the homeless. My whole approach had always been to try to offer services to get them working, and to help them become free of addictions. Over the years, because I had met so many homeless people, I had developed a deep fondness towards them. Do you know why?

I have learned that if you really pay attention, every person you meet has something to teach you. Yes, "even" the homeless have something to teach all of us. It is amazing! Many people, when they see a homeless person, think that they are dirty, nasty, and useless. Yet, every time I stood and talked to one, they would give me a gem of wisdom. They would offer something that would literally blow my mind, showing me how wise they were. And sometimes, while I'm talking to them, even if they were drunk, or high on some type of a drug, I was learning from them.

So, on this day, holding this five dollar bill, I had a decision to make. Do I give all of it to this gentleman in front of me right now? Then a thought came through my mind. Let me bless this money, with my mind, and let him use the five dollars for his highest good, whatever that might be. In an instant, I decided to hand him the money.

As I handed the money to him, I said, "You know, I hope that this will be enough to get you home."

He took the money, said thank you, turned and walked away. Then he turned back to me and said, "Hey!"

I turned around, and he said, "This is a five dollar bill!"

I started laughing. "I know. Normally, I give you a dollar, but this is the only money I have, so this must be what you need."

"Well, I can't accept a five dollar bill without giving you something in return!"

I thought to myself, "Oh, my gosh! What does that mean? What's he going to do, give me a hug? I don't know if I even want something from him in return."

"No, no that's fine," I said, "Just take your five dollars. But use it for something good. I want to make this point really clear. When I handed you that five dollar bill, I gave it to you with the intention that you would use it for your highest good. So, use that money for something good."

He then looked at me and said, "Well, ok, listen. I can't accept five dollars without giving you something back. So, I wanna offer you this deal."

I started laughing, thinking, "A deal! A homeless guy is going to offer me a deal for the five dollars I just gave him?"

As we both stood there looking at each other, I said, "Ok, what's the deal?"

"Here it is!" he said, "I love to tell stories. So, in exchange for this five dollar bill I'm gonna tell you this story."

And with that, I nodded and said, "Go right ahead."

In this book is the story that Mark, the homeless person, shared with me that day. Of course, I added a few extra points to help the story along, but the ideas here definitely began with the amazing tale that Mark offered to me in exchange for my five dollar bill. I am blessed to this day, that I was able to stop and listen to his story, the one you are about to read. Yes, the homeless men and women in this world are blessed by God, too.

Let's begin.

ROCK STAR!

Finding God's Purpose for Your Life

By David Essel, M.S.

with help from Mark, the homeless man

CHAPTER 1

We Meet a Rock

A very, very, very long time ago, in the middle of a desert land, lived a group of rocks and stones.

Now, many of us think of rocks and stones as being, well, just rocks and stones! In other words, they don't have any feelings, thoughts or personalities. But do you know what? That's not always the case! For in this desert land, there was one very special rock, about the size of the palm of your hand, and that rock had a dream.

That's right! Rocks have dreams! They want to be used for something. They want to have an exciting life, just like you and I do. Now many people don't know this to be true, but I can tell you it is true. There is not one thing made on this earth by God that does not have a divine purpose.

Do you realize that? Yes, everything on earth has a divine purpose, a purpose for being here. Even trees have a divine purpose. Some are here to be the homes for animals, while others are here to be made into houses to give us shelter. Some are here to stand tall to help produce the oxygen that keeps us all alive and well. They all have a purpose in life.

Well, in this far away desert land, the rock knew he had an ultimate purpose in life to make a difference in this world. He didn't know what that purpose was, but he knew he was divinely placed, exactly where he was supposed to be. To be divinely used in some unique and special way.

For years the rock had an incredible dream! He woke up every day excited about finding his purpose here on earth. "I wonder, how am I going to be used? How am I going to make a difference in this world?" he thought. Patiently, day by day, he sat and waited, excited to see why he was here on earth.

Around our rock friend were all kinds of other rocks and stones. Some were really big, while others were really tiny. And they all had dreams, too. But none could compare to this one rock's dreams.

CHAPTER 2

Footsteps In The Desert

Years and years and years went by and all of a sudden there were footsteps in the desert. Now, let me tell you something! This desert was so desolate and barren, that these rocks and stones had never heard footsteps until this one day.

The rock got really excited and started vibrating in the sand. He was so excited because it meant that if there were footsteps, that there were people coming! Could today be the day that he would discover why he was here on earth, he wondered?

Before the rock knew it, there were even more footsteps. The rock could sense that some of the other rocks and stones around him were being picked up and being used to build a home, right in the middle of the desert! But it wasn't an ordinary home. It was a stone castle!

The rock was so excited, because he knew that somewhere along the wall of this home, this rich merchant's home, that he would be used to fulfill his divine purpose on earth. Today was going to be his lucky day!

But as all the footsteps kept going around and around and picking up all the other rocks and stones, this one rock was never touched. Days came and days went. Weeks came and weeks went. And while all the other stones around him were being picked up and used to make this beautiful castle in the desert, our rock friend was never chosen.

Then all of the footsteps began to fade away. And the rock started to get very, very, depressed. I don't know if you have ever seen what a depressed rock looks like, but oh my Lord, he was a sad looking rock!

Our rock friend became so depressed, that he started sinking into the sand. He was giving up hope. The sand started to cover him over. And as he sank deeper and deeper into the sand, he kept asking the question, "Am I not good enough to be used for some divine purpose on this earth? I thought I had a calling. I remember one time, for years, I had a dream. I would wake up every morning, excited, about what I was going to do here on this earth. But, maybe I was wrong."

Throughout the days and weeks that followed, the sand covered up the rock. And everyday, when he would wake up, he knew he was covered with more and more sand. One day, he thought to himself, "I guess I'm not as special as I hoped I was."

But, even as the weeks and months and years went by, something was staying alive in the rock. In his heart was one little place, filled with a spark of light that would not go out. And no matter how depressed the rock got, there was one little speck of light, of Spirit in his soul that begged, "Don't give up."

CHAPTER 3

Never Give Up

One morning, the rock decided to pay attention to the inner voice that kept saying, "Don't give up, you are special." He started to shake and shimmy and vibrate himself back up from all the sand that covered him, until he reached the surface of the desert once again. He could tell that he reached the surface, because for the first time in years he felt the sun shining on his face! The rock was getting excited and wanted to start exploring his dreams all over again.

His faith, in himself, was starting to return. The rock thought, "You know, I do have a purpose. And I know that even though years have gone by and all the other rocks and stones around me have been used to build this huge, beautiful castle in the middle of the desert, that it's my turn now. I know that God put me here for a divine purpose and I am going to find out what it is!

I am going to wake up every day and pray to God, "How would you like to use me, God? What is my divine purpose here? Lord, how is it that I can be of service to you here, now?"

So, every day, the rock, about the size of the palm of your hand, continued to pray over and over. The little rock's spirit was lifted. And every day, when the sun would rise and shine and warm the rock in the desert, he started praying to God, "Praise God! Praise the Lord! How would you like to use me? I know that I am part of your divine plan God. How would you like to use me?"

And throughout the day, the rock just praised God over and over and over again. And when night would come, the rock would quiet down with a big smile on his little rock face. Then he would tuck himself in, cover himself with some extra sand, and go to sleep for the night. And the next day as the warm sun came and shone upon the rock, he would get excited and praise God all day long. This went on for days, and then for months and months and months. The rock never stopped praising God.

CHAPTER 4

The People Return

While nothing outstanding was happening yet in his life, this rock had faith. Then, one day, from out of nowhere, the rock began to hear footsteps again. The remaining rocks that had not been used to build the castle were being used to build the wall to protect the castle. Now, our friend the rock was getting excited all over again!

"Yes! I knew my prayers would be answered! Yes! I knew my prayers would be answered! Praise God! Praise God! My prayers are being answered! I'm going to be used as part of the wall to protect the castle."

He yelled out, "Pick me! Pick me!" as the footsteps were racing around picking up all the other stones, making this glorious wall around the castle. The little rock screamed out, as loud as he could, "Pick me! Pick me! Praise God! Pick me! Pick me! Praise God! Today is my day! I will be used, my divine purpose to be a rock, to be a part of the wall, protecting the castle. Pick me!"

Days went by and all the other stones were being picked up. They were cheering with joy, because they were going to be a part of the wall that was protecting the castle.

After a period of time, the little rock started to get depressed again. There were less and less footsteps. The workers were fewer and fewer and our friend the rock was once again, feeling all alone in the desert.

As the sun set, the rock started sinking into the sand again. All the excitement about finding his divine purpose in life, all the excitement about serving God, all of his praising God, seemed once again unanswered. His dreams about being used as a part of the great wall that protected the magnificent castle in the desert seemed all for nothing.

The rock started to think, once again, "Maybe I don't have a special purpose after all."

About a week or two of sadness went by before the rock caught the depressed feeling that was coming over him. All of his rock and stone friends were used for the great wall, for a high and mighty purpose, and he realized he hadn't been chosen again. Somehow though, that little spark inside his heart, that little spark of soul, the little spark of spirit, started to come to life again.

He said to himself, "You know what? I'm not going to get depressed again. I'm not going to sink into the sand. I'm going to stay on the surface. I'm going to be here, ready for God when God is ready to use me."

CHAPTER 5

The Return of Faith

Sometimes, life seems hard. Sometimes, it may even feel like all of our friends are gone. We question, "What's the purpose of living?" And it seems like there is no purpose. We think, "Maybe I'm not that special after all." And this is when we need to praise God even more. We need to have faith!

The rock started thinking about the past. "When I used to listen to the rocks and stones around me talk about faith, they would say that faith in God is most important when things are tough! When times seem to be difficult, when friends are leaving, that's when I need to be praising God even more. And the more we praise God, the better our chances of finding our divine purpose after all. "

So now, when the sun came up every day, our friend the rock was sitting in the sun, praising God for the opportunity to serve Him, when the time was right.

"Is today my day, God? Is this when you want to use me?" He repeated the phrase day after day, after day.

Weeks and months went by, and not a sound was heard in the desert. The weeks and months turned into years without a sound in the desert. The rock knew that the only way he would find his divine purpose was with the help of men, because men would use him in the glory of God for his divine purpose. So, he kept his faith up. The sun would rise, and he would praise God. As the sun set every day, he would have a smile on his little rock face. As our rock friend went to sleep at night, he knew that God's purpose for his life was right around the corner.

Now many times in life, when things aren't going our way, it's hard to have a good attitude. When our grades in school aren't the best, when we don't make the sports team or the cheerleading squad, when our best friend leaves us to be the best friend of someone else, it can be really hard to have great faith in God. When our family breaks up or we lose our job, keeping our spirits high can be a very hard thing to do. When our health is failing or we are battling addictions, having "faith" can seem an impossible task.

During these challenging times, God wants us to dig deep into our heart and soul, and to be grateful for all that we do have. That's what it means to have faith! Faith is simply believing in the things that have not yet come into our lives.

CHAPTER 6

A Giant In The Desert

Well, the little rock decided to practice this theory. Week after week and month after month went by and our friend the rock stayed strong. He stayed solid in his faith. And then one day, he heard huge footsteps in the desert! I mean, the biggest footsteps ever! As a matter of fact, tremors went through the sand, with every step of this monster, this person, this giant coming towards the rock! The rock could feel the sand shift, and the earth shake.

At first the rock thought, "We're having an earthquake! Those footsteps are causing an earthquake all around me!"

And then all of a sudden, the huge footsteps stopped, about fifty yards in front of the rock.

The rock thought, "Thank goodness, I guess the earthquake is over with."

A minute or two later, he heard tiny footsteps come up and circle around him. The next thing he knew, the footsteps stopped right next to him. He said, "That's interesting! The earthquake stopped and now there is a young person doing circles around me."

As quickly as it had stopped, the earth started shaking again. Those huge footsteps were coming towards him, and when they were about twenty-five yards away, they stopped.

The next thing he knew, he heard those two small footsteps right next to him.

"Oh my gosh! There's someone towering over me," he thought.

CHAPTER 7

The Rock Becomes A Star

After a few more moments, there was silence in the desert. And before he knew it he was picked up off the ground! The rock almost jumped out of his rock skin with excitement! The rock was finally picked up for the first time in his life. A human being, a man had picked up the rock!

The rock said to himself, "Yes! I'm going to be used. Yes, I'm going to finally find my divine purpose. Praise God! Praise God! I know now that I'm going to find out what my destiny is today."

With that last thought, the rock felt himself being twirled around in a circle, faster and faster and faster. And the rock kept saying, "Yes! Use me for my divine purpose, God. Yes, use me for your purpose."

Over and over again, the rock was being spun in super fast circles! Faster and faster and faster, he twirled, and then, as quickly as it all started, he was thrown through the air!

The little rock was now flying through the air, faster than a rocket! He was traveling so fast he could not believe it! And the whole time, the rock kept saying, "Thank you God, I praise you God, you have found my work in this world. My destiny has been reached. I don't know where I'm going, and I don't know why I am flying God, but I thank you!"

And just as the rock said his final thank you to God, BAM! He crashed into what felt like a huge mountain. "What did I just hit? What did I run into?" thought the rock.

And with that, the rock fell to the desert and landed in the hot sand. For what seemed like an eternity later, he sat there wondering, "Is this it? Is this all I was here for? Is my life's work done? Completed? Over? That quickly?"

Then, the mightiest crash happened right next to the rock! What seemed to be a huge earth-quake shook the desert sand once again! And then, there was stillness.

All of a sudden, the rock heard the cheer of a nation, a full army screaming in victory!

And the rock had no idea what has just happened.

A few seconds later, a young boy came over and picked up the rock. His name was David.

The rock's purpose was to be the rock that David, King David of Israel, who is written about multiple times in the bible, used in his sling to throw through the air, to kill the mighty giant Goliath. Goliath, who stood over ten feet tall, was a huge warrior from a nation that had repeatedly threatened the lives of David's people.

The warrior Goliath was killed by the rock. Our rock! Our friend the rock became a star!

CHAPTER 8

God Has Big Plans for Each Of Us

David carried that rock home and kept it with him for the rest of his life. The rock, who for years and years, never thought he had much of a purpose in life, found out that he did have a purpose, a divine purpose. He was the rock that King David used to slay the giant Goliath.

Yes, God's plan for our "Rock Star" was much bigger than anything he could have dreamed of. As the rock sat day after day in King David's pocket, he continued to praise God over and over and over. And of course, he did it with a beautiful smile that spread across his little rock face.

Our friend the rock, who started out living the life of what many would believe to be nothing more than an ordinary, simple, desert rock, finally found his purpose in life and yes, lived happily ever after. He found the "promised land", Heaven On Earth, right here, right now.

As he laid on the table at the foot of King David's bed, he let out a little rock yawn, and started to fall asleep for the night.

Then, out of the corner of his eye, he saw a beautiful, small rose colored stone, with a smile on her little face, sitting on King David's night stand. As he opened his eyes wider, he saw that she was staring right back at him!

"Oh yes!" he thought, "that is the most beautiful rose colored stone I have ever seen in my life! And she's looking right at me! My goodness, I think she just winked at me!"

Could our little rock star have another purpose in life?

Could a new adventure for our friend be in the making?

Only time will tell.

As they say, God often works in mysterious ways!

THE END

SUMMARY

When we think about this story, we can ask ourselves these questions:

Do I really believe that I have a divine purpose? Please explain.

_____

_____

_____

_____

_____

_____

Do I really know that I have been given special gifts and talents to use and serve God with? What are my talents? What do I love to do? What brings me joy?

_____

_____

_____

_____

_____

_____

How am I like the rock, the star of God's plan, to take down a mighty giant that was threatening David?

_____

_____

_____

_____

_____

_____

Is there something in my life that I think might be holding me back? What is the Goliath in my life?

_____

_____

_____

_____

_____

_____

Can I be stronger in my faith like the rock, when things aren't going my way? How?

_____

_____

_____

_____

_____

_____

What steps can I take today to deepen my faith in God's plan for my life?

_____

_____

_____

_____

_____

_____

Am I willing to believe that God has a purpose for my life? Please explain.

_____

_____

_____

_____

_____

_____

What could I do differently in my life today to become the "Star" God wants me to be?

_____

_____

_____

_____

iii

_____

_____

Who could help me deepen my faith in my life and in God today?

_____

_____

_____

_____

_____

_____

How can I help other people overcome their blocks in life?

_____

_____

_____

_____

_____

_____

Every boy, every girl, every man, and every woman on this earth, has been put here with divine gifts and talents that can be used to serve God and each other, but only if we believe that this is true for all of us.

Sometimes our personal gifts are hidden for years. But if we keep the faith, if we trust in God and our faith is strong, we will be shown how to use our gifts to serve God, just like our friend the rock.

Let's all be the "rock stars" of our own lives. Let's be the "rock stars" in the eyes of God. God already knows we are. Do you know this, too?

Let's go ahead and fulfill his purpose by keeping the faith and moving forward and doing the good work, the great work, the divine work of God, every day of our lives.

Let's show other people how strong our faith is every day, so we can help them build the same faith for themselves, as well.

Let's show other people compassion and love, forgiveness and friendship, so when they are down and depressed, then we can be that savior in their lives, too.

Every one of us has a divine purpose. Let's go ahead and explore that today by deepening our faith in our loving God.

We hope you have thoroughly enjoyed David's sixth book "Rock Star!" As he would say if he was speaking to you right now, please take a moment before any more time passes, and answer the questions at the end of the book in writing. The process of slowing down, and taking the time to answer these life changing questions, will help you to get the most out of your life, starting today!

If you would like to bring David in as an inspirational speaker to your business, group, or non profit, please contact him at www.davidessel.com, or call 941.266.7676.

From everyone at David Essel Inc, we wish you a blessed and blissful day!

DAVID ESSEL, M.S.,

Author, Adjunct Professor, Radio/TV Host, Master Life/Relationship Coach, Inspirational Speaker, Addiction Recovery Coach, All Faiths Minister

http://www.davidessel.com
(Free information on personal growth and more!)

http://www.lifecoachuniverse.com
(See Certification Programs offered below.)

http://www.youtube.com/superslowdown
(300 Free Videos: Inspiration/Love)

13010 Metro Parkway, Ft. Myers Florida, 33966

PHONE: 941.266.7676

Teleconference Sessions and Workshops: The World

Certification Programs offered for: Life Coach, Public Speaking, Spirituality, and Holistic Addiction Recovery

Slow Down Blog:
http://davidesselblog.blogspot.com/

Join us on Facebook:
http://www.facebook.com/davidesselalive

HOOPS FOR HOMELESS VETERANS

In 2011 David Essel created, "Hoops for Homeless Veterans", a project to help raise funds and awareness for those who have served our country, and now need our assistance.

The statistics are sad, and shocking. According to Veteran Affairs, nearly 200,000 veterans are homeless in the USA on any given night. As documented in the "2009 Challenge Report", in the state of Florida alone, there are only 450 funded beds to treat homeless veterans, while there are over 18,000 homeless veterans in the entire state in need of our help!

David's "Hoops for Homeless" project is an event in which he performs 1000 consecutive basketball free throws and invites the community, media and sponsors to get involved. David is available to come into other cities, to do this fundraising event for the homeless veterans, as well as other homeless people. If you would like to make a difference in your community, with the homeless population, David would love to help you create a, "Hoops for Homeless"...fundraiser in your city.

Twenty-five cents from the sale of every book will be donated to homeless shelters for men and women across the USA.

58483011R00045

Made in the USA
Charleston, SC
11 July 2016